Editor
Gisela Lee, M.A.

Managing Editor
Karen Goldfluss, M.S. Ed.

Editor-in-Chief
Sharon Coan, M.S. Ed.

Illustrator
Howard Chaney

Cover Artist
Barb Lorseyedi

Art Director
CJae Froshay

Art Coordinator
Kevin Barnes

Imaging
Temo Parra

Product Manager
Phil Garcia

Publisher
Mary D. Smith, M.S. Ed.

Math Review
GRADE 4

Author

Patricia Miriani Sima

Teacher Created Resources, Inc.
6421 Industry Way
Westminster, CA 92683
www.teachercreated.com

ISBN-0-7439-3744-9

©2003 Teacher Created Resources, Inc.
Reprinted, 2006
Made in U.S.A.

Table of Contents

Introduction 3

Practice 1: time measurement 4

Practice 2: time measurement 5

Practice 3: time measurement 6

Practice 4: time measurement 7

Practice 5: rounding/estimating numbers 8

Practice 6: money .9

Practice 7: basic geometry 10

Practice 8: charts and graphs 11

Practice 9: charts and graphs 12

Practice 10: standard form of writing
numbers 13

Practice 11: expanded form of writing
numbers 14

Practice 12: place value 15

Practice 13: addition and subtraction 16

Practice 14: basic geometry 17

Practice 15: basic geometry 18

Practice 16: basic geometry 19

Practice 17: basic geometry 20

Practice 18: basic geometry 21

Practice 19: basic geometry 22

Practice 20: basic geometry 23

Practice 21: basic geometry 24

Practice 22: decimals 25

Practice 23: fractions and decimals 26

Practice 24: fractions 27

Practice 25: fractions 28

Practice 26: ordinal numbers 29

Practice 27: ordinal numbers 30

Practice 28: multiplication and division 31

Practice 29: measurement 32

Practice 30: order of operations 33

Practice 31: prime numbers 34

Practice 32: factorization 35

Practice 33: basic math review 36

Practice 34: probability 37

Practice 35: word problems 38

Practice 36: statistical analysis 39

Test Practice 1 40

Test Practice 2 41

Test Practice 3 42

Test Practice 4 43

Test Practice 5 44

Test Practice 6 45

Answer Sheet 46

Answer Key 47

Introduction

The old adage "practice makes perfect" can really hold true for your child and his or her education. The more practice and exposure your child has with concepts being taught in school, the more success he or she is likely to find. For many parents, knowing how to help their children can be frustrating because the resources may not be readily available. As a parent it is also difficult to know where to focus your efforts so that the extra practice your child receives at home supports what he or she is learning in school.

This book has been designed to help parents and teachers reinforce basic skills with children. *Practice Makes Perfect* reviews basic math skills for children in grade 4. The focus is a review of math skills. While it would be impossible to include all concepts taught in grade 4 in this book, the following basic objectives are reinforced through practice exercises. These objectives support math standards established on a district, state, or national level. (Refer to Table of Contents for specific objectives of each practice page.)

- adding and subtracting
- multiplying and dividing
- adding and subtracting money
- using a number line
- using a calendar

- using fractions
- using standard form
- finding the perimeter
- finding important information
- using time

There are 36 practice pages. (*Note*: Have children show all work where computation is necessary to solve a problem. For multiple choice responses on practice pages, children can fill in the letter choice or circle the answer.) Following the practice pages are six test practices. These provide children with multiple-choice test items to help prepare them for standardized tests administered in schools. As your child completes each test, he or she can fill in the correct bubbles on the optional answer sheet provided on page 46. To correct the test pages and the practice pages in this book, use the answer key provided on pages 47 and 48.

How to Make the Most of This Book

Here are some useful ideas for optimizing the practice pages in this book:

- Set aside a specific place in your home to work on the practice pages. Keep it neat and tidy with materials on hand.

- Set up a certain time of day to work on the practice pages. This will establish consistency. Look for times in your day or week that are less hectic and more conducive to practicing skills.

- Keep all practice sessions with your child positive and more constructive. If the mood becomes tense, or you and your child are frustrated, set the book aside and look for another time to practice with your child.

- Help with instructions if necessary. If your child is having difficulty understanding what to do or how to get started, work through the first problem with him or her.

- Review the work your child has done. This serves as reinforcement and provides further practice.

- Allow your child to use whatever writing instruments he or she prefers. For example, colored pencils can add variety and pleasure to drill work.

- Pay attention to the areas in which your child has the most difficulty. Provide extra guidance and exercises in those areas. Allowing children to use drawings and manipulatives, such as coins, tiles, game markers, or flash cards, can help them grasp difficult concepts more easily.

- Look for ways to make real-life applications to the skills being reinforced.

Practice 1

Using a Calendar

Complete the calendar.

January

Sunday	Monday	Tuesday	Wednesday	Thursday	Friday	Saturday
		1				
				31		

Use the calendar to answer the questions.

1. January 10 is a _____.

2. There are _____ days in January.

3. There are _____ full weeks in this month.

4. The second Tuesday is the _____.

5. There are _____ Sundays in January.

6. There are _____ days between in January 3rd and January 11th.

7. The day after January 9th is the _____.

8. The last Saturday in January is the _____.

What measure of time should you use?

9. summer vacation	days	weeks	months	years
10. age	days	weeks	months	years
11. bean seed sprouting	days	weeks	months	years
12. a school year	days	weeks	months	years
13. a tree growing	days	weeks	months	years
14. school carnival	days	weeks	months	years

Practice 2

Shuttle Express Schedule

Stops	Departs	Arrives	Travel Time
1. Main Street to Park Street	8:03	8:10	_____ min.
2. Park Street to Box Street	8:10	8:22	_____ min.
3. Box Street to Market Street	8:22	8:31	_____ min.
4. Market Street to Barrel Street	8:31	8:39	_____ min.
5. Barrel Street to Main Street	8:39	8:45	_____ min.

Use the schedule to answer the questions.

6. Which route has the longest travel time?

_____ to _____ has the longest travel time.

7. Which route has the shortest travel time?

_____ to _____ has the shortest travel time.

8. Where is the shuttle at 8:25?

The shuttle is on the _____ to _____ route.

9. How many minutes does it take the shuttle to go to every stop?

It takes the shuttle _____ minutes.

10. If you need to take the shuttle to Market Street from Box Street, what time do you need to be at the shuttle stop?

I need to be at the shuttle stop by _____.

Practice 3

To the Minute

Write the time that each clock shows.

1.    2.    3.    4.

_____   _____   _____   _____

Read each word problem. Write the elapsed time.

5. Dale leaves for school at 9:10. He arrives at school at 9:19.

   Elapsed time: _____ minutes.

6. Regina put the cookies in the oven at 9:20. She took the cookies out at 9:37.

   Elapsed time: _____ minutes.

7. Edna began playing the piano at 10:10 and finished at 10:45.

   Elapsed time: _____ minutes.

8. Garrett started cleaning the tub at 2:34 and finished at 2:59.

   Elapsed time: _____ minutes.

9. Tovias left the library at 2:10 and arrived back home by 2:55.

   Elapsed time: _____ minutes.

10. Ruby left for the mall at 6:31 and reached the mall at 6:57.

    Elapsed time: _____minutes.

11. June put the pizza in the oven at 6:09 and took it out of the oven at 6:55.

    Elapsed time: _____ minutes.

12. Josiah began making pancakes for breakfast at 5:21 and finished at 5:40.

    Elapsed time: _____ minutes.

Practice 4

Fractions of Time

Write the number of minutes.

1. an hour = _____ minutes

2. half an hour = _____ minutes

3. quarter of an hour = _____ minutes

4. one-tenth of an hour = _____ minutes

5. one-twelfth of an hour = _____ minutes

In the Kitchen: Setting the Timer

Answer each question.

6. How long should Danielle bake the cake?

    1 second   1 minute   1 hour
     ○   ○   ○

7. How long should Mario cook the spaghetti?

    10 seconds   10 minutes   10 hours
     ○   ○   ○

8. How long should Brandon bake the cookies?

    12 seconds   12 minutes   12 hours
     ○   ○   ○

9. How long should Louisa wash the carrots?

    30 seconds   30 minutes   30 hours
     ○   ○   ○

10. How long should Bianca pour juice into a glass?

    3 seconds   3 minutes   3 hours
     ○   ○   ○

11. How long should Vince cook each pancake?

    2 seconds   2 minutes   2 hours
     ○   ○   ○

Practice 5 ੭ ☺ ੭ ☺ ੭ ☺ ੭ ☺ ੭ ☺ ੭ ☺ ੭ ☺ ੭ ☺

Rounding Numbers

When rounding to the nearest hundred, look at the number in the tens place. If the number is 5 or larger, round up. If the number is less than 5, round down. Round each number to the nearest hundred.

1. 469 _____   **2.** 104 _____   **3.** 440 _____   4. 892 _____

Read each word problem. Round the numbers to the nearest hundred. Then add or subtract to estimate the sum or difference.

5. Rodney had 552 Canadian coins and 279 English coins. How many coins does he have in all?

6. Olivia had 801 German coins and 80 French coins. How many coins does she have in all?

7. Elliot had 106 Russian coins and 340 Austrian coins. How many coins does he have in all?

_____

_____

_____

8. Amy's motorcycle trip is 699 miles. She has ridden 380 miles. How many more miles are needed to complete her trip?

9. Matt's bicycle trip is 981 miles. He has ridden 176 miles. How many more miles are needed to complete his trip?

10. Erin's airplane trip is 349 miles. She has flown 153 miles. How many more miles are needed to complete her trip?

_____

_____

_____

11. Add the set of numbers. Rewrite the same math problem using numbers rounded to the nearest hundred. How do the two answers compare?

```
  123      _____        The answers are: _____
  473      _____
+  95    + _____        _____
```

Practice 6

Rounding Money

When rounding money to the nearest dollar, look at the number in the tenths place—the first number to the right of the decimal (.) point. If the number is 5 or greater, round up. If the number is less than 5, round down.

1. $7.18 _____   2. $1.01 _____   3. $5.71 _____   4. $6.96 _____

When rounding money to the nearest ten dollars, look at the number in the ones place. If the number is 5 or greater, round up. If the number is less than 5, round down.

5. $23.70 _____   6. $24.22 _____   7. $27.80 _____

Round the price of each item to the nearest dollar and write the math problem. Add or subtract.

 $4.75

 $.64

 $5.59

 $10.41

 $55.27

8. Add.

+ _____

9. Subtract.

− _____

10. Subtract.

− _____

11. Add.

+ _____

Practice 7

Line, Line Segment, or Ray?

Identify each figure as a line segment or ray.

1.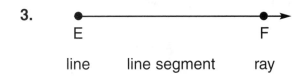
    A   B

    line   line segment   ray

2. C   D

    line   line segment   ray

3. E   F

    line   line segment   ray

4. G   H

    line   line segment   ray

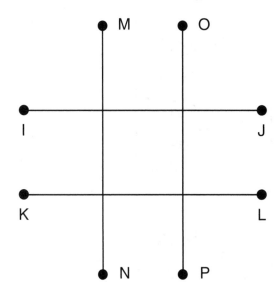

Answer each statement.

5. $\overline{IJ}$ is parallel to _____.

6. $\overline{KL}$ intersects _____

   and _____.

7. $\overline{MN}$ is parallel to _____.

8. $\overline{OP}$ intersects _____ and

   _____.

9. $\overline{OP}$ is not parallel to _____

   or _____.

10. $\overline{MN}$ does not intersect _____.

11. $\overline{IJ}$ does not intersect _____.

12. Write $\overline{MN}$ another way.

   _____

Practice 8

Automotive Vehicles Sold

Make a horizontal bar graph showing the following information.

 Sports Cars   61,917   Small Trucks   38,214

 Vans   41,945   Big Trucks   43,127

 Station Wagons   73,958   SUV's   29,060

 Family Cars   62,000   Small Cars   54,498

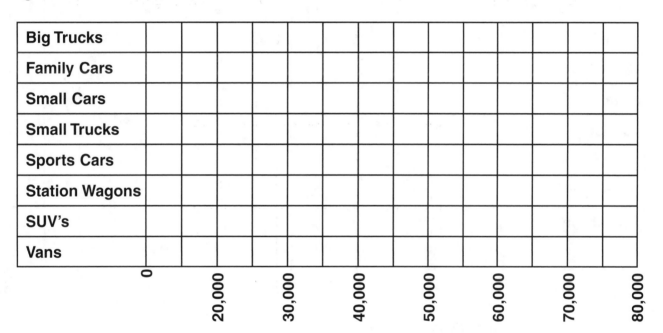

Big Trucks								
Family Cars								
Small Cars								
Small Trucks								
Sports Cars								
Station Wagons								
SUV's								
Vans								

0   20,000   30,000   40,000   50,000   60,000   70,000   80,000

Find the sums and the differences.

1. Small Trucks + Big Trucks = _____

2. Sports Cars + Small Cars = _____

3. Station Wagons + Family Cars = _____

4. SUV's + Vans = _____

5. Small Trucks – SUV's = _____

6. Family Cars – Small Cars = _____

7. Sport Cars – Big Trucks = _____

8. Station Wagons – Vans = _____

Practice 9

Favorite Family Vacation Spots

Make a horizontal bar graph showing the following information.

Beach	68,585	Camping	51,541
Road Trip	47,371	Big City	21,230
Mountains	32,371	Cruise	65,460
Stay Home	10,111	Another Country	16,221

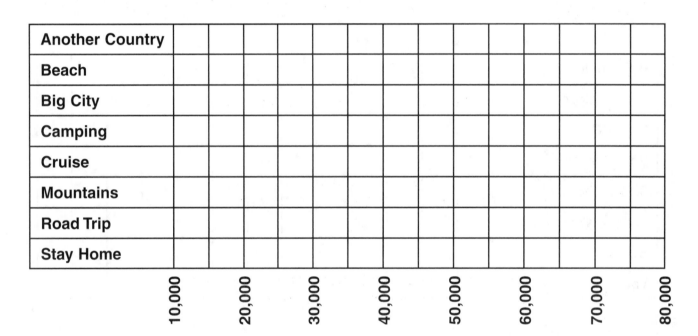

Find the sums or the differences.

1. Beach + Stay Home = _____

2. Mountains + Camping = _____

3. Road Trip + Big City = _____

4. Cruise + Another Country = _____

5. Another Country – Stay Home = _____

6. Road Trip – Mountains = _____

7. Beach – Cruise = _____

8. Camping – Big City = _____

Practice 10

Populations

Write each country's population in standard form.

1. Belle lives in the Bahamas. The population is two hundred ninety-four thousand, nine hundred eighty-two.

_____

2. Han's family lives in Austria. The population is eight million, one hundred thirty-one thousand, one hundred eleven.

_____

3. Val visited Vanuatu. The population is one hundred eighty-nine thousand, six hundred eighteen.

_____

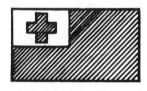

4. Tommy once visited Tonga. The population is one hundred two thousand, three hundred twenty-one.

_____

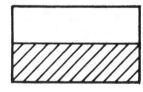

5. Tina once traveled to San Marino. The population is twenty-six thousand, nine hundred thirty-seven.

_____

Using the information above, answer the questions below.

6. Which country has the smallest population? _____

7. Which country has the largest population? _____

8. Which country has a population larger than Tonga and smaller than the Bahamas?

_____

9. Which country is the third largest?_____

10. Which country is the second smallest? _____

Practice 11

Expanded Notation: Using Words

Rewrite each state's square kilometers (km) in expanded form.

	Millions	Hundred Thousands	Ten Thousands	Thousands	Hundreds	Tens	Ones
1. Wyoming		2	5	3	3	4	9
2. Alaska	1	5	2	2	5	9	6
3. Indiana			9	3	7	2	0
4. Arizona		2	9	5	2	7	6
5. California		4	1	0	8	9	6
6. Rhode Island				3	1	4	2

Example: Wyoming—two hundred fifty-three thousand, three hundred forty-nine km

1. Rhode Island _____

_____

2. Alaska _____

_____

3. Indiana _____

_____

4. California _____

_____

5. Arizona _____

Practice 12 ⟳ ⟲ ⟳ ⟲ ⟳ ⟲ ⟳ ⟲ ⟳ ⟲ ⟳ ⟲ ⟳ ⟲ ⟳

Wheel of Numbers

Use a paper clip as the "spinner" and the end of a pencil to hold it in place. Spin the spinner, record the number, write the number that is in the specific place value, and round the number to the number specified in the place value.

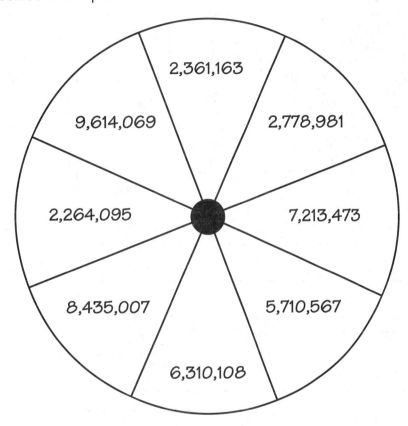

	Number	Place Value	Number	Rounded to the Nearest Place Value Indicated
Ex:	9,614,069	tens	6	9,614,070
1.		hundreds		
2.		thousands		
3.		ten thousands		
4.		hundred thousands		
5.		millions		
6.		thousands		
7.		hundred thousands		
8.		millions		

Practice 13 ๑ ๑ ๑ ๑ ๑ ๑ ๑ ๑ ๑ ๑ ๑ ๑ ๑ ๑ ๑ ๑ ๑ ๑

Secret Message

Add or subtract. Write the letter that goes with each answer on the line to reveal a secret message.

1.	2.	3.	4.
810,842 890,013 + 105,831 = O	964,116 − 106,115 = A	260,303 − 173,992 = Y	472,574 299,748 + 616,325 = C
5.	6.	7.	8.
204,582 − 170,425 = R	580,590 131,226 + 890,304 = S	935,365 461,342 + 915,762 = N	875,718 − 469,958 = U
9.	10.	11.	
500,581 − 487,643 = L	169,748 171,071 + 167,011 = !	237,114 − 193,357 = T	

—— —— ——
1,602,120 858,001 86,311

—— ——
2,312,469 1,806,686

—— —— —— —— —— —— —— —— —— —— —— —— —— ——
43,757 1,806,686   1,388,647 858,001 12,938 1,388,647 405,760 12,938 858,001 43,757 1,806,686 34,157 1,602,120 507,830

Practice 14

Symmetry

If an object can be folded in half (or fourths) and all of the sections match exactly, the object is said to be symmetrical. Look at each picture and decide if all of the sections are the same.

1. 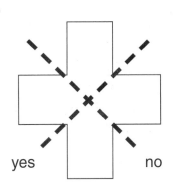 yes no	2. 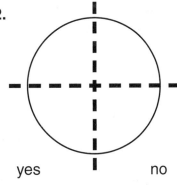 yes no	3. 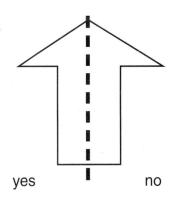 yes no
4. 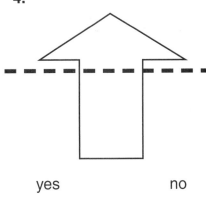 yes no	5. 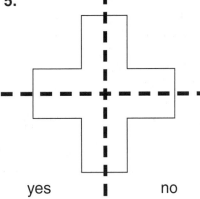 yes no	6. 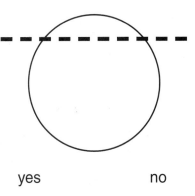 yes no

Draw the line of symmetry to make the number of equal parts.

7. 2 parts

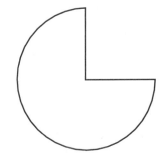

8. 4 parts

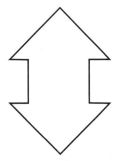

9. 8 parts

Practice 15

Plane Figures and Solids

Draw a line matching each plane figure to its solid figure.

Circle	Rectangle	Triangle	Square

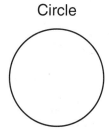 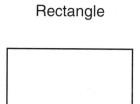 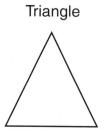 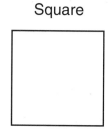

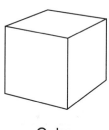 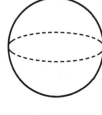 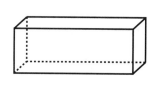 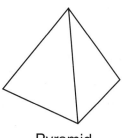

Cube	Sphere	Rectangular Prism	Pyramid

Make a list of all of the things in the room that match each solid figure.

Cube	Sphere	Rectangular Prism	Pyramid
1. _____	1. _____	1. _____	1. _____
2. _____	2. _____	2. _____	2. _____
3. _____	3. _____	3. _____	3. _____
4. _____	4. _____	4. _____	4. _____
5. _____	5. _____	5. _____	5. _____
6. _____	6. _____	6. _____	6. _____
7. _____	7. _____	7. _____	7. _____
8. _____	8. _____	8. _____	8. _____
9. _____	9. _____	9. _____	9. _____
10. _____	10. _____	10. _____	10. _____

Practice 16

A Triangle by Any Other Name Is Still a Triangle

Triangles can be identified in two ways, by their angles or by their sides. Match each triangle to its definition.

Sides

Angles

Equilateral

All sides are the same length.

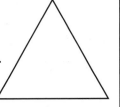

Acute

All angles are < 90°.

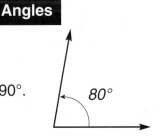

Isosceles

Two sides are the same length.

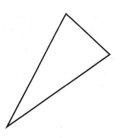

Right

One angle is = 90°.

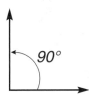

Scalene

None of the sides are the same length.

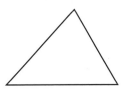

Obtuse

An angle is > 90°.

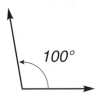

1. Draw a scalene triangle.

3. Draw a triangle with a right angle.

2. Draw an isosceles triangle.

4. Draw an obtuse triangle.

Practice 17

Rotation

rotation 0°   rotation 90°   rotation 180°   rotation 270°   rotation 360°

How many degrees has each object been rotated (turned)? Circle the answer.

1.	2. 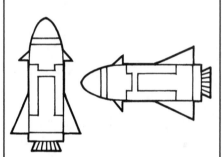	3. 
0°/360° 180° 90° 270°	0°/360° 180° 90° 270°	0°/360° 180° 90° 270°
4. 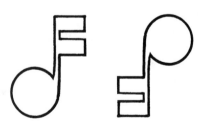	5. 	6.
0°/360° 180° 90° 270°	0°/360° 180° 90° 270°	0°/360° 180° 90° 270°

Practice 18

Circles

Identify the parts of a circle.

_____ **1.** Circumference is the distance around the circle.

_____ **2.** The center is in the middle of the circle.

_____ **3.** The radius is a line from the center of the circle to any points on the outside edge of the circle.

_____ **4.** The diameter is the joining of two radii on the same line.

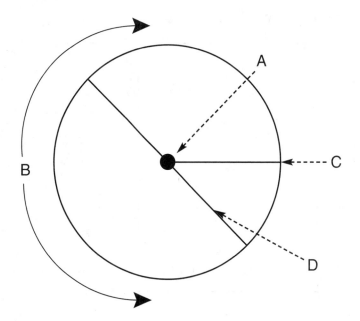

Measure the distance of the radius of each circle. Then draw the radius for each circle.

5.

The radius is _____ cm..

6.

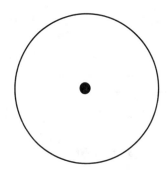

The radius is _____ cm.

7. .

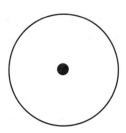

The radius is _____ cm.

8.

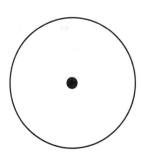

The radius is _____ cm.

Practice 19

Name That Angle!

Name each angle two ways.

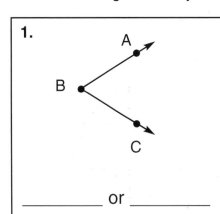

1.	2.	3.
_____ or _____	_____ or _____	_____ or _____

Name each angle by writing right, acute, or obtuse.

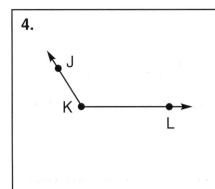 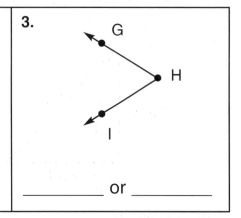

4.

_____

5.

_____

6.

_____

Congruence

Objects are congruent when they are the same shape and size.

7. Are they congruent? yes   no

8. Are they congruent? yes   no

9. Draw two shapes that are the same size but not the same shape.

10. Draw two shapes that are the same shape but not the same size.

Practice 20

Finding the Perimeter

The perimeter is the distance around a shape. Find the perimeter for each shape.
(Remember, to find the perimeter, add the lenghts of all the sides.)

1.

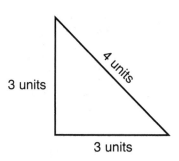

The perimeter is

___ + ___ + ___ = ___ square units.

2.

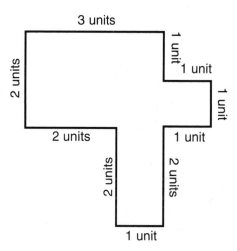

The perimeter is ___ + ___ + ___ + ___ + ___

___ + ___ + ___ + ___ + ___ = ___ square

units.

3.

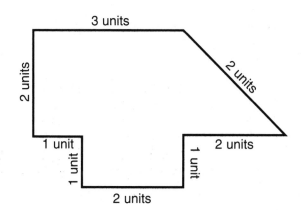

The perimeter is ___ + ___ + ___ + ___

___ + ___ + ___ + ___ = ___ square units.

4. Draw a shape with a perimeter of 19
square units.

Practice 21

Finding the Area of Squares and Rectangles

Find the area for each problem.

1.

1 m

6 m

A = _____

2.

10 in.

12 in.

A = _____

3.

8 cm

A = _____

4.

8 ft.

2 ft.

A = _____

5.

6 in.

3 in.

A = _____

6.

7 ft.

5 ft.

A = _____

7.

80 m

50 m

A = _____

8.

90 cm

20 cm

A = _____

Practice 22

Ordering Decimals

Write the decimals in order from smallest to largest.

1. 0.39, 0.56, 0.75, 0.31 _____, _____, _____, _____

2. 0.59, 0.35, 0.67, 0.37 _____, _____, _____, _____

3. 1.12, 4.78, 6.74, 1.70 _____, _____, _____, _____

4. 10.04, 90.22, 62.34, 35.69 _____, _____, _____, _____

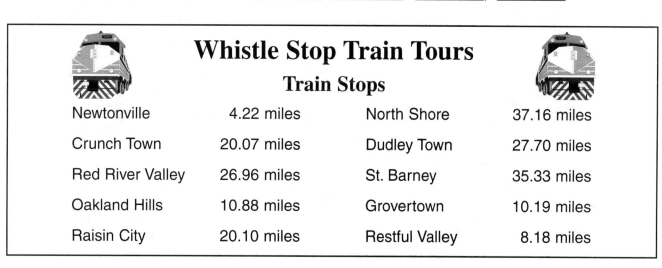

Whistle Stop Train Tours
Train Stops

Newtonville	4.22 miles	North Shore	37.16 miles
Crunch Town	20.07 miles	Dudley Town	27.70 miles
Red River Valley	26.96 miles	St. Barney	35.33 miles
Oakland Hills	10.88 miles	Grovertown	10.19 miles
Raisin City	20.10 miles	Restful Valley	8.18 miles

Write the towns in order from closest to farthest.

5. Restful Valley, Raisin City, North Shore

_____, _____, _____

6. Oakland Hills, Dudley Town, Crunch Town

_____, _____, _____

7. North Shore, St. Barney, Grovertown

_____, _____, _____

8. Red River Valley, Dudley Town, North Shore

_____, _____, _____

9. Restful Valley, Oakland Hills, St. Barney

_____, _____, _____

10. Newtonville, St. Barney, Raisin City

_____, _____, _____

Practice 23

Fractions and Decimals

Rewrite each fraction as a decimal.

1. Seline has 1/4 of a dollar.

_____

2. Jorge ate 1/2 of the hamburger.

_____

3. Sherry ate 3 of the 4 strawberries.

_____

Rewrite each decimal as a fraction.

4. Who ate .25 of the cake?

_____

5. Alexis can find only 50 of a pair of shoes.

_____

6. Dana ate .75 of the 8 cookies.

_____

Compare each fraction and decimal, using >, <, or = .

7.

.50 ◯ $\frac{3}{4}$

8.

.25 ◯ $\frac{1}{2}$

9.

.75 ◯ $\frac{1}{4}$

Use the number line to compare negative numbers. Use the > (greater than) or < (less than) symbols.

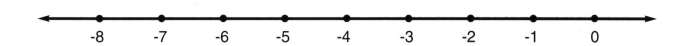

10.

-1 ◯ -7

11.

-10 ◯ -8

12.

-6 ◯ -2

13.

-8 ◯ -7

14.

-5 ◯ -1

15.

-4 ◯ 0

Practice 24

Simplifying Fractions

Simplify each fraction to its lowest term.

1.

$\frac{6}{9}$ = _____

2.

$\frac{4}{8}$ = _____

3.

$\frac{6}{8}$ = _____

4.

$\frac{6}{12}$ = _____

Finish each equivalent fraction pattern.

5. 1/2, 2/4, 3/6, 4/8, _____, _____, _____, _____

6. 1/3, 2/6, 3/9, 4/12, _____, _____, _____, _____

7. 1/4, 2/8, 3/12, 4/16, _____, _____, _____, _____

8. 1/1, 2/2, 3/3, 4/4, _____, _____, _____, _____

Better Goods Bakery

Buy the correct number of baked goods.

| cheesecake | cupcakes | cinnamon rolls | croissants | cookies | pretzels |

9. 1/6 of a dozen cupcakes = _____ cupcakes

10. 1/4 of a dozen pretzels = _____ pretzels

11. 3/4 of a dozen cookies = _____ cookies

12. 1/3 of a dozen cinnamon rolls = _____ cinnamon rolls

13. 2/3 of a dozen croissants = _____ croissants

14. 1/2 of 4 cheesecakes = _____ cheesecakes

Practice 25

Adding and Subtracting Fractions

Add or subtract.

1. $\begin{array}{r} \frac{3}{7} \\ + \frac{1}{9} \\ \hline \end{array}$	**2.** $\begin{array}{r} \frac{3}{7} \\ + \frac{1}{6} \\ \hline \end{array}$	**3.** $\begin{array}{r} \frac{1}{9} \\ + \frac{1}{10} \\ \hline \end{array}$
2. $\begin{array}{r} \frac{3}{7} \\ + \frac{1}{9} \\ \hline \end{array}$	**2.** $\begin{array}{r} \frac{3}{7} \\ + \frac{1}{9} \\ \hline \end{array}$	6. $3/7 - 2/9$ $\begin{array}{r} \frac{3}{7} \\ + \frac{1}{9} \\ \hline \end{array}$

Color the fractions that have been reduced to their simplest forms.

$\frac{3}{7}$	$\frac{1}{4}$	$\frac{2}{3}$	$\frac{4}{7}$	$\frac{2}{8}$	$\frac{3}{7}$
$\frac{1}{3}$	$\frac{1}{8}$	$\frac{2}{6}$	$\frac{2}{9}$	$\frac{3}{6}$	$\frac{1}{5}$
$\frac{6}{9}$	$\frac{1}{2}$	$\frac{1}{9}$	$\frac{4}{5}$	$\frac{2}{4}$	$\frac{4}{8}$

Practice 26

Ordered Pairs

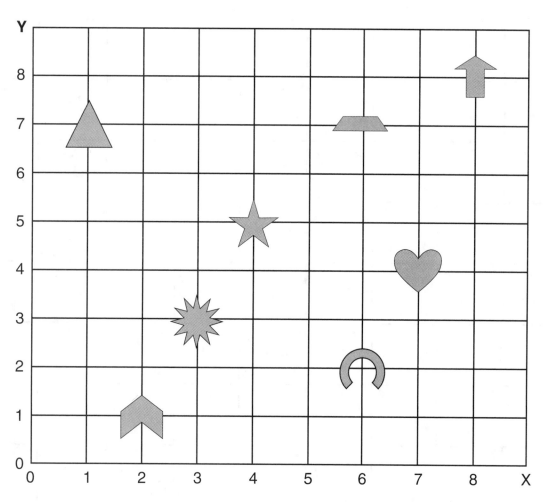

XWhat item is in each location?

Example: (2, 1) Go over 2 spaces and up 1 space.

1. (8, 8)   2. (3, 3)

3. (1, 7)   4. (6, 7)

Where is each item located? Circle the correct ordered pair.

5.   (4, 5)   (7, 4)   6.   (2, 1)   (6, 2)

Practice 27

Coordinate Points

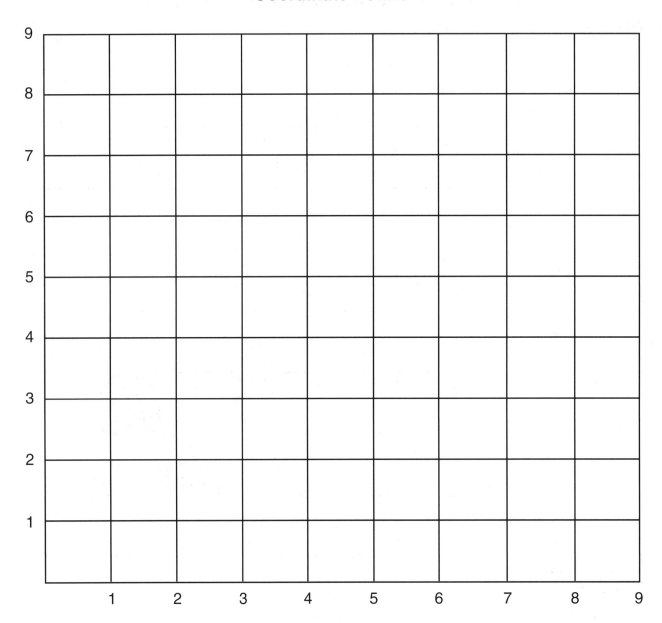

Make a circle in each location. Connect the circles in order to make a shape.

(2, 2), (3, 4), (1, 6), (3, 6), (4, 8), (5, 6), (7, 6), (5, 4), (6, 1), (4, 3) and connect it to (2, 2)

What shape did you make? _____

Practice 28

Multiplication and Division Crossword Puzzle

Write the answer to each problem.

Across

2. 713 x 73

5. 802 x 16

6. 1,134 ÷ 18

7. 256 ÷ 16

8. 3,105 x 29

10. 990 ÷ 99

11. 974 x 50

12. 2,496 ÷ 16

Down

1. 756 ÷ 63

3. 4,430 ÷ 10

4. 6,710 x 60

5. 4,031 ÷ 29

9. 687 x 68

10. 100 ÷ 10

Practice 29 ✺ ✺ ✺ ✺ ✺ ✺ ✺ ✺ ✺ ✺ ✺ ✺

How Many Miles?

Convert each distance from kilometers (km) to miles (mi.).

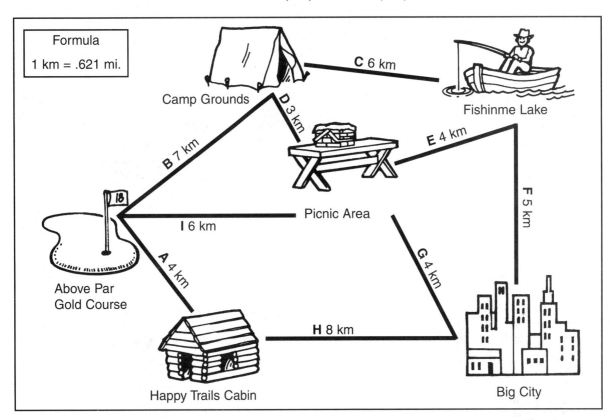

Formula
1 km = .621 mi.

Camp Grounds

C 6 km

Fishinme Lake

D 3 km

B 7 km

E 4 km

F 5 km

Picnic Area

I 6 km

Above Par
Gold Course

A 4 km

G 4 km

H 8 km

Happy Trails Cabin

Big City

1. Happy Trails Cabin to Big City _____ km _____ mi.

2. Fishinme Lake to Picnic Area _____ km _____ mi.

3. Above Par Gold Course to Camp Grounds _____ km _____ mi.

List the different routes that could be taken to go from Above Par Golf Course to
Fishinme Lake.

4. _____ = _____ km _____ mi.

5. _____ = _____ km _____ mi.

6. _____ = _____ km _____ mi.

7. _____ = _____ km _____ mi.

8. Which route is the longest? _____

9. Which route is the shortest? _____

10. Are there any routes that are about the same in distance? _____

Practice 30 ꙮ ꙮ ꙮ ꙮ ꙮ ꙮ ꙮ ꙮ ꙮ ꙮ ꙮ ꙮ ꙮ ꙮ

Order of Operations

Do the operation in (parentheses) first.

1. $(6 \times 3) \div 2$	2. $(3 \times 2) \div 6$	3. $(2 \times 6) \div 3$
4. $(8 \div 4) \times 2$	5. $(5 + 2) \times 4$	6. $(4 \div 2) \times 8$

Solve each word problem.

7. Lily had 10 jellybeans evenly distributed into 5 plastic sandwich bags. Her sister Billie had twice the number of jellybeans than in one of Lily's bags. How many jellybeans did Billie have in one bag?

   Billie had _____ jellybeans in one bag.

8. Grady had 10 jellybeans evenly distributed into 2 plastic sandwich bags. His brother Brady had 5 times the number of jellybeans than in one of Grady's bags. How many jellybeans did Brady have in one bag?

   Brady had _____ jellybeans in one bag.

Practice 31

Prime Numbers

A **prime number** is any whole number greater than 1 that has only its own number and the number 1 as its factors.

Example: 3 is a prime number. Its only factors are 3 and 1 (3 x 1 = 3).

4 is not a prime number. Its factors are 1 x 4 and 2 x 2.

Look at each pair of numbers. Circle the number that is a prime number.

1. 7 6	**2.** 5 10	**3.** 2 9	**4.** 6 11
5. 4 13	**6.** 39 19	**7.** 27 13	**8.** 33 41
9. 17 25	**10.** 3 49	**11.** 37 14	**12.** 12 29
13. 15 23	**14.** 21 11	**15.** 31 18	**16.** 27 47

Practice 32

Name Those Factors!

Write the factors for each product.

Example: 6 (6 can be made by 1 x 6, 2 x 3)

The factors are 1, 2, 3, and 6.

1. 4	2. 16	3. 10

Write the factors for each number.

4. Melody's favorite number is 32.	5. Jimmy's favorite number is 60.
6. Terri's favorite number is 18.	7. Brent's favorite number is 9.
8. Sunny's favorite number is 12.	9. Nile's favorite number is 15.

Practice 33

Missing Signs and Numbers

Each set of numbers has the same number added, subtracted, divided, and multiplied. Write the missing sign and number.

1.

Missing Number _____		
sign	862	863
	5,900	5,900
	4,200	4,199
	27	27

2.

Missing Number _____		
sign	556	553
	63	21
	192	195
	4,310	12,930

3.

Missing Number _____		
sign	17	85
	755	151
	140	135
	3,481	3,486

4.

Missing Number _____		
sign	2,934	2,944
	370	3,700
	1,000	100
	1,214	1,204

Practice 34

Build-It-Yourself Backpacks

How many different kinds of backpacks can be made using the following choices? (Only one item from each category at a time can be used in building each new backpack design.)
(**Note:** There may be more combinations possible than available spaces. If that is the case, use the space on the back of this page.)

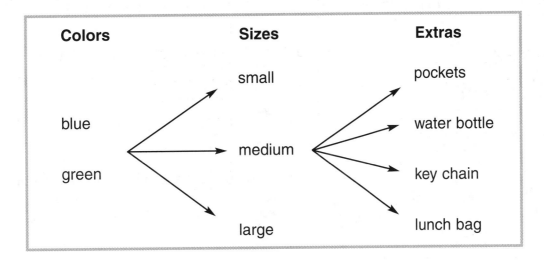

Backpacks

Style #	Color	Size	Extras
Example	blue	small	pockets
#1			
#2			
#3			
#4			
#5			
#6			
#7			
#8			
#9			
#10			
#11			
#12			

Practice 35 ꙮ ꙮ ꙮ ꙮ ꙮ ꙮ ꙮ ꙮ ꙮ ꙮ ꙮ ꙮ ꙮ

Missing Information

What piece of information is needed to solve the problem?

Example: Benito went to the bakery and bought 6 cupcakes and some cookies. How many cookies did Benito buy?

Question to ask: *How many items did Benito purchase in all? (Number of items – cupcakes = number of cookies.)*

1. Makayla has $10.00. Does she have enough to buy a soccer ball and a pair of shin guards?

   _____

   _____

2. Minnie's class is going on a field trip. Each bus can take 20 kids. How many buses does Minnie's class need?

   _____

   _____

3. Garth picked the same number of grapes as the combined total of plums and peaches. How many grapes did Garth pick?

   _____

   _____

4. Jennifer bought a bag of jellybeans. There were 23 red jellybeans and 15 orange jellybeans. The rest were black jellybeans. How many black jellybeans were in the bag?

   _____

   _____

5. Cerise needs to put 10 seeds in each pot. How many seeds does Cerise need?

   _____

   _____

6. Oliver earned 10 more points on the spelling test than Guy. What was Oliver's score?

   _____

   _____

Practice 36

Pancake Breakfast Fund Raiser

Make a horizontal bar graph using the following information.

Roscoe ate 6 pancakes.   Rhett ate 10 pancakes.

Laverne ate 3 pancakes.   Buddy ate 1 pancake.

Kelsey ate 2 pancakes.   Carmella ate 4 pancakes.

Cara ate 4 pancakes.   Gage ate 7 pancakes.

Irene ate 4 pancakes   May ate 6 pancakes.

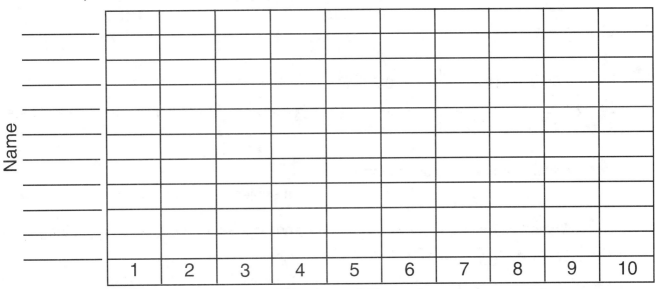

Number of Pancakes

Find the mean (average) number of pancakes eaten by the students.

1. Add the number of pancakes eaten.

   _____ + _____ + _____ + _____ + _____ + _____ + _____ + _____ + _____ + _____
   = _____ pancakes

2. Divide the total number of pancakes eaten by the number of students.

   _____ (pancakes) ÷ _____ (students) = _____

3. The mean is _____ pancakes.

Find the median. The median is the middle number between the most number of pancakes eaten and the fewest number of pancakes eaten.

4. _____ (most number) + _____ (fewest number) = _____ ÷ 2 = _____

Find the mode. The mode is the number of pancakes eaten that occurred most frequently.

5, The mode is _____ pancakes.

Test Practice 1

1. Round to the nearest dollar.

$1.86

$1.80 $1.90 $2.00

Ⓐ   Ⓑ   Ⓒ

2. How many minutes are in 2 hours?

60   90   120

Ⓐ   Ⓑ   Ⓒ

3. How many minutes are in a quarter of an hour?

5   10   15

Ⓐ   Ⓑ   Ⓒ

4. What is the time?

11:09   10:09   12:09

Ⓐ   Ⓑ   Ⓒ

5. Round to the nearest ten dollars.

$10.23

$9.00 $10.00 $11.00

Ⓐ   Ⓑ   Ⓒ

6. Round to the nearest hundred.

798

700   800   900

Ⓐ   Ⓑ   Ⓒ

Use the schedule to answer the questions.

Class Schedule	
8:05–8:30	Computers
8:30–8:45	Spelling
8:45–10:00	Reading
10:00–10:15	Recess
10:15–11:15	Math
11:15–12:00	Writing
12:00–1:45	Lunch
1:45–2:15	P.E.
2:15–2:45	Art

7. What subject is taught at 9:00?

Reading   Spelling   Art   Math

Ⓐ   Ⓑ   Ⓒ   Ⓓ

8. What time is lunch?

12:00   10:00   8:00   1:00

Ⓐ   Ⓑ   Ⓒ   Ⓓ

9. How long is P.E.?

15 min.   30 min.   45 min.   25 min.

Ⓐ   Ⓑ   Ⓒ   Ⓓ

10. How many minutes are spent working on computers?

5 min.   15 min.   25 min.   30 min.

Ⓐ   Ⓑ   Ⓒ   Ⓓ

Test Practice 2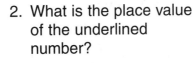

1. What is the place value of the underlined number?

   2,<u>5</u>81,066

   million   ten   one
     (A)   (B)   (C)

2. What is the place value of the underlined number?

   1,23<u>6</u>,748

   hundred   ten   thousand
     (A)   (B)   (C)

3. What is the place value of the underlined number?

   8,478,<u>3</u>80

   ten   hundred   one
   (A)   (B)   (C)

---

4. Identify the object.

   A   B

   line   line segment   ray
   (A)   (B)   (C)

5. Identify the object.

   A   B

   line   line segment   ray
   (A)   (B)   (C)

---

6. Identify the object.

   E   F

   line   line segment   ray
   (A)   (B)   (C)

7. Identify the relationship of the two lines.

   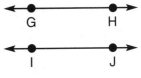
   G   H

   I   J

   parallel   perpendicular   intersecting
     (A)   (B)   (C)

---

8. Add.

   $$\begin{array}{r} 76{,}720 \\ 10{,}414 \\ +\ 38{,}316 \end{array}$$

   152,450   215,540   125,450
     (A)   (B)   (C)

9. Subtract.

   $$\begin{array}{r} 99{,}910 \\ -\ 19{,}715 \end{array}$$

   80,195   90,195   10,915
    (A)   (B)   (C)

#3744 Practice Makes Perfect: Math Review

Test Practice 3

1. Identify the rotation.

90°	180°	270°	60°
Ⓐ	Ⓑ	Ⓒ	Ⓓ

2. Which arrow shows a 360° rotation?

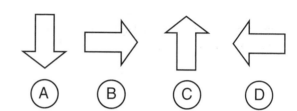

Ⓐ	Ⓑ	Ⓒ	Ⓓ

3. Is it symmetrical?

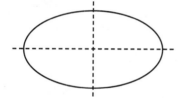

yes	no
Ⓐ	Ⓑ

4. Name the angle.

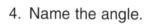

acute	obtuse	right
Ⓐ	Ⓑ	Ⓒ

5. Name the triangle.

equilateral	isosceles	scalene
Ⓐ	Ⓑ	Ⓒ

Identify the parts of a circle.

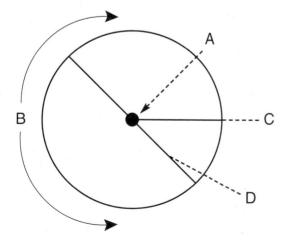

6. Name the circumference.

A	B	C	D
Ⓐ	Ⓑ	Ⓒ	Ⓓ

7. Name the center.

A	B	C	D
Ⓐ	Ⓑ	Ⓒ	Ⓓ

8. Name the diameter.

A	B	C	D
Ⓐ	Ⓑ	Ⓒ	Ⓓ

Test Practice 4

1. Identify the smallest decimal.

   .14   .20   .03

   Ⓐ   Ⓑ   Ⓒ

2. Identify the largest decimal.

   .14   .20   .03

   Ⓐ   Ⓑ   Ⓒ

3. Reduce 4/8 to its simplest form.

   1/4   2/8   1/2

   Ⓐ   Ⓑ   Ⓒ

4. Find the perimeter.

  16 units   24 units   20 units

   Ⓐ   Ⓑ   Ⓒ

5. What is 1/3 of a dozen?

   3   4   6

   Ⓐ   Ⓑ   Ⓒ

6. Find the area. (area = 1 x w)

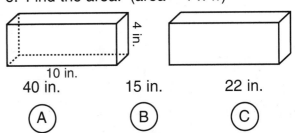

  40 in.   15 in.   22 in.

   Ⓐ   Ⓑ   Ⓒ

7. Find the volume. (area = s x s)

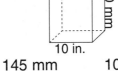 

 145 mm   100 mm   160 mm

   Ⓐ   Ⓑ   Ⓒ

8. Add.

        1/2 + 1/4

  2/4   3/4   1/8

   Ⓐ   Ⓑ   Ⓒ

9. Subtract.

        3/5 − 1/4

  7/20   2/5   4/5

   Ⓐ   Ⓑ   Ⓒ

10. Which is the largest?

  .25   3/4   .025

   Ⓐ   Ⓑ   Ⓒ

Test Practice 5

Find each shape's location.

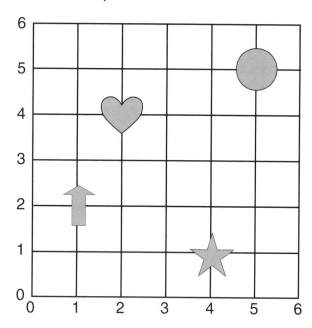

1. Where is the heart?

(4, 2)	(2, 4)	(4, 1)	(1, 4)
Ⓐ	Ⓑ	Ⓒ	Ⓓ

2. Where is the star?

(4, 1)	(1, 5)	(1, 4)	(1, 2)
Ⓐ	Ⓑ	Ⓒ	Ⓓ

3. Which is farther away?

(1 km = .621 miles)

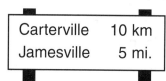

Carterville   10 km
Jamesville   5 mi.

Carterville	Jamesville
Ⓐ	Ⓑ

4. Identify the missing sign.

75 ☐ 3 = 25

+	x	÷	–
Ⓐ	Ⓑ	Ⓒ	Ⓓ

5. Which operation should be done first?

(4 x 10) – 19 = ?

4 x 10	10 – 19	4 x 19	4 – 19
Ⓐ	Ⓑ	Ⓒ	Ⓓ

6. Identify the math sentence.

Reggie made 18 cookies. He sold 9 of them at his cookie stand. His sister, Gina sold three times as many cookies as Reggie. How many cookies did Gina, Sell?

(18 – 3) x 9	(18 – 9) x 3
Ⓐ	Ⓑ

18 x (9 – 3)	(18 x 3) – 9
Ⓒ	Ⓓ

Test Practice 6 ৹ ৺ ৹ ৺ ৹ ৺ ৹ ৺ ৹ ৺ ৹ ৺

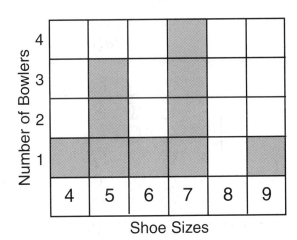

Number of Bowlers

Shoe Sizes

Use the graph above to answer questions 1 and 2

1. What was the mean (average) shoe size?

   6.0   6.1   6.2   6.3
   (A)   (B)   (C)   (D)

2. What was the median (middle number) shoe size?

   6.0   6.5   7.0   7.5
   (A)   (B)   (C)   (D)

3. Identify the factors for 24.

   (A) 1, 2, 3, 4, 5, 6, 7, 8
   (B) 1, 2, 3, 4, 6, 8, 12, 24
   (C) 1, 2, 3, 4, 6, 10, 12, 14
   (D) 1, 2, 3, 4, 6, 10, 12

4. Divide.

   $4\overline{)880}$

   (A) 110   (C) 330
   (B) 220   (D) 440

5. Identify the prime numbers.

   (A) 3, 4, 5, 7
   (B) 3, 4, 7, 9, 11
   (C) 3, 5, 7, 11
   (D) 2, 4, 7, 8

6. Multiply.

   $575 \times 9 = \boxed{}$

   (A) 5,175   (C) 5,075
   (B) 5,200   (D) 5,275

7. Multiply.

   $\frac{7}{15} \times \frac{1}{2} = \boxed{}$

   (A) $\frac{7}{30}$ (C) $\frac{8}{17}$
   (B) $\frac{14}{15}$ (D) $\frac{6}{13}$

8. What information is missing?

   Leonard's birthday is coming soon. The party will be at the park and will last 2 hours. Cake and punch will be served. What time will the party be over?

   (A) What time will the party start?
   (B) Where will the party be held?
   (C) When will the party be held?
   (D) How long did the party last?

Answer Sheet

Test Practice 1	Test Practice 2	Test Practice 3
1. Ⓐ Ⓑ Ⓒ	1. Ⓐ Ⓑ Ⓒ	1. Ⓐ Ⓑ Ⓒ Ⓓ
2. Ⓐ Ⓑ Ⓒ	2. Ⓐ Ⓑ Ⓒ	2. Ⓐ Ⓑ Ⓒ Ⓓ
3. Ⓐ Ⓑ Ⓒ	3. Ⓐ Ⓑ Ⓒ	3. Ⓐ Ⓑ
4. Ⓐ Ⓑ Ⓒ	4. Ⓐ Ⓑ Ⓒ	4. Ⓐ Ⓑ Ⓒ
5. Ⓐ Ⓑ Ⓒ	5. Ⓐ Ⓑ Ⓒ	5. Ⓐ Ⓑ Ⓒ
6. Ⓐ Ⓑ Ⓒ	6. Ⓐ Ⓑ Ⓒ	6. Ⓐ Ⓑ Ⓒ Ⓓ
7. Ⓐ Ⓑ Ⓒ Ⓓ	7. Ⓐ Ⓑ Ⓒ	7. Ⓐ Ⓑ Ⓒ Ⓓ
8. Ⓐ Ⓑ Ⓒ Ⓓ	8. Ⓐ Ⓑ Ⓒ	8. Ⓐ Ⓑ Ⓒ Ⓓ
9. Ⓐ Ⓑ Ⓒ Ⓓ	9. Ⓐ Ⓑ Ⓒ	
10. Ⓐ Ⓑ Ⓒ Ⓓ		

Test Practice 4	Test Practice 5	Test Practice 6
1. Ⓐ Ⓑ Ⓒ	1. Ⓐ Ⓑ Ⓒ Ⓓ	1. Ⓐ Ⓑ Ⓒ Ⓓ
2. Ⓐ Ⓑ Ⓒ	2. Ⓐ Ⓑ Ⓒ Ⓓ	2. Ⓐ Ⓑ Ⓒ Ⓓ
3. Ⓐ Ⓑ Ⓒ	3. Ⓐ Ⓑ	3. Ⓐ Ⓑ Ⓒ Ⓓ
4. Ⓐ Ⓑ Ⓒ	4. Ⓐ Ⓑ Ⓒ Ⓓ	4. Ⓐ Ⓑ Ⓒ Ⓓ
5. Ⓐ Ⓑ Ⓒ	5. Ⓐ Ⓑ Ⓒ Ⓓ	5. Ⓐ Ⓑ Ⓒ Ⓓ
6. Ⓐ Ⓑ Ⓒ	6. Ⓐ Ⓑ Ⓒ Ⓓ	6. Ⓐ Ⓑ Ⓒ Ⓓ
7. Ⓐ Ⓑ Ⓒ		7. Ⓐ Ⓑ Ⓒ Ⓓ
8. Ⓐ Ⓑ Ⓒ		8. Ⓐ Ⓑ Ⓒ Ⓓ
9. Ⓐ Ⓑ Ⓒ		
10. Ⓐ Ⓑ Ⓒ		

Page 4
Missing Numbers: 2–30

1. Thursday
2. 31
3. 3
4. 8th
5. 4
6. 7
7. 10th
8. 26th
9. months
10. years
11. days
12. months
13. years
14. days

Page 5
1. 7 min.
2. 12 min.
3. 9 min.
4. 8 min.
5. 6 min.
6. Park Street to Box Street
7. Barrel Street to Main Street
8. Box Street to Market Street
9. 42 min.
10. 8:22

Page 6
1. 10:04
2. 4:48
3. 8:16
4. 6:39
5. 9 min.
6. 17 min.
7. 35 min.
8. 25 min.
9. 45 min.
10. 26 min.
11. 46 min.
12. 19 min.

Page 7
1. 60 min.
2. 30 min.
3. 15 min.
4. 6 min
5. 5 min.
6. 1 hour
7. 10 min.
8. 12 min.
9. 30 seconds
10. 3 seconds
11. 2 min.

Page 8
1. 500
2. 100
3. 400
4. 900
5. 300 + 600 = 900 coins
6. 800 + 100 = 900 coins
7. 100 + 300 = 400 coins
8. 700 − 400 = 300 miles
9. 1,000 − 200 = 800 miles
10. 300 − 200 = 100 miles
11. 123 + 473 + 95 = 691 and
    100 + 500 + 100 = 700

Sample Sentence: The answers are very close to each other.

Page 9
1. $7
2. $1
3. $6
4. $7
5. $20
6. $20
7. $30
8. $6 + $5 + $10 = $21
9. $7 − $1 − $5 = $1
10. $60 − $50 − $1 = $9
11. $55 + $1 + $6 = $62

Page 10
1. Line
2. Line Segment
3. Ray
4. Line
5. KL or LK
6. MN or NM and OP or PO
7. OP or PO
8. IJ or JI and KL or LK
9. IJ/JI or KL/LK
10. OP or PO
11. KL or LK
12. NM

Page 11

Big Trucks								
Family Cars								
Small Cars								
Small Trucks								
Sports Cars								
Station Wagons								
SUV's								
Vans								

(10,000 20,000 30,000 40,000 50,000 60,000 70,000 80,000)

1. 81,341
2. 116,415
3. 135,958
4. 71,005
5. 9,154
6. 7,502
7. 18,790
8. 32,013

Page 12

Another Country								
Beach								
Big City								
Camping								
Cruise								
Mountains								
Road Trip								
Stay Home								

(10,000 20,000 30,000 40,000 50,000 60,000 70,000 80,000)

1. 78,696
2. 83,912
3. 68,601
4. 81,681
5. 6,110
6. 15,000
7. 3,125
8. 30,311

Page 13
1. 294,982
2. 8,131,111
3. 189,618
4. 102,321
5. 26,937
6. San Marino
7. Austria
8. Vanuatu
9. Vanuatu
10. Tonga

Page 14
1. Three thousand, one hundred forty-two
2. One million, five hundred twenty-two thousand, five hundred ninety-six
3. Ninety-three thousand, seven hundred twenty
4. Four hundred ten thousand, eight hundred ninety-six
5. Two hundred ninety-five thousand, two hundred seventy-six

Page 15
Answers will vary.

Page 16
1. 1,806,686
2. 858,001
3. 86,311
4. 1,388,647
5. 34,157
6. 1,602,120
7. 2,312,469
8. 405,760
9. 12,938
10. 507,830
11. 43,757

Secret Message: Say no to Calculators!

Page 17
1. yes
2. yes
3. yes
4. no
5. yes
6. no

Page 18
Circle-Sphere
Rectangle-Rectangular Prism
Square-Cube
Triangle-Pyramid
Lists: Answers will vary.
Sample answers for cube: desk, Kleenex box, toy box
Sample answers for sphere: different kinds of balls, head, globe
Sample answers for rectangular prism: pencil box, reading book, lunch pail
Sample answers for pyramid: wooden blocks, a toy structure (tinker toys, a hat)

Page 20
1. 90°
2. 270°
3. 0°/360°
4. 180°
5. 90°
6. 90°

Page 21
1. B
2. A
3. C
4. D
5. 1 cm
6. 2 cm
7. 1.5 cm
8. 1.75 cm

Page 22
1. <ABC or <CBA
2. <DEF or <FED
3. <GHI or <IHG
4. obtuse
5. right
6. acute
7. no
8. yes
9. Shapes will vary.
10. Shapes will vary.

Page 23
1. 10 square units
2. 16 square units
3. 14 square units
4. Shapes will vary.

Page 24
1. 6 m^2
2. 120 in.^{2}
3. 64 cm^2
4. 16 ft.^{2}
5. 18 in.^{2}
6. 35 in.^{2}
7. 4,000 m^2
8. 1,800 cm^2

Answer Key

Page 25
1. .31, .39, .56, .75
2. .35, .37, .59, .67
3. 1.12, 1.70, 4.78, 6.74
4. 10.04, 35.69, 62.34, 90.22
5. Restful Valley, Raisin City, North Shore
6. Oakland Hills, Crunch Town, Dudley Town
7. Grovertown, St. Barney, North Shore
8. Red River Valley, Dudley Town, North Shore
9. Restful Valley, Oakland Hills, St. Barney
10. Newtonville, Raisin City, St. Barney

Page 26
1. $0.25
2. .5
3. .75
4. 1/4
5. 1/2
6. 3/4
7. <
8. <
9. >
10. >
11. <
12. <
13. <
14. <
15. <

Page 27
1. 2/3
2. 1/2
3. 3/4
4. 1/2
5. 5/10, 6/12, 7/14, 8/16
6. 5/15, 6/18, 7/21, 8/24
7. 5/20, 6/24, 7/28, 8/32
8. 5/5, 6/6, 7/7, 8/8
9. 2 cupcakes
10. 3 pretzels
11. 9 cookies
12. 4 cinnamon rolls
13. 8 croissants
14. 2 cheesecakes

Page 28
1. 34/63
2. 5/6
3. 1/90
4. 12/10 or 1 2/10 or 1 1/5
5. 5/8
6. 13/63
Top Row: 3/7, 1/4, 2/3, 4/7, 3/7
Middle Row: 1/3, 1/8, 2/9, 1/5
Bottom Row: 1/2, 1/9, 4/5

Page 29
1. arrow
2. starburst
3. triangle
4. trapezoid
5. (4, 5)
6. (6, 2)

Page 30
The shape is a star.

Page 31
Across
2. 52,049
5. 12,832
6. 63
7. 16
8. 90,045
10. 10
11. 48,700
12. 156
Down
1. 12
3. 443
4. 402,600
5. 139
9. 46,716
10. 10

Page 32
1. 8 km, 4.968 mi.
2. 4 km, 2.484 mi.
3. 7 km, 4.247 mi.
4.–7. sample answers: Road I and Road E 6 km + 4 km = 10 km or .621 mi.; Road A, Road H, Road G, Road E 4 + 8 + 4 + 4 km = 20 km or 12.42 mi.; Road A, Road H, Road F 4 + 8 + 5 = 17 km or 10.557 mi.; Road B and Road C 7 + 6 = 13 km or 8.037 mi.
8.–10. Answers will vary depending upon the selected routes.

Page 33
1. 9
2. 1
3. 4
4. 4
5. 28
6. 16
7. 4
8. 25

Page 34
1. 7
2. 5
3. 2
4. 11
5. 13
6. 19
7. A
8. C

Page 35
1. 1 x 4, 2 x 2
2. 1 x 16, 2 x 8, 4 x 4
3. 1 x 10, 2 x 5
4. 1 x 32, 2 x 16, 4 x 8
5. 1 x 60, 2 x 30, 3 x 20, 4 x 15, 5 x 12, 6 x 10
6. 1 x 18, 2 x 9, 3 x 6
7. 1 x 9, 3 x 3
8. 1 x 12, 2 x 6, 3 x 4
9. 1 x 15, 3 x 5

Page 36
1. Missing number is 1; +1; x 1; − 1; ÷ 1
2. Missing number is 3; − 3; ÷ 3; + 3; x 3
3. Missing number is 5; x 5; ÷ 5; − 5; + 5
4. Missing number is 10; + 10; x 10; ÷ 10; − 10

Page 37
Sample answers:
1. blue (or green), small, water bottle
2. blue (or green), small, key chain
3. blue (or green), small, lunch bag
4. blue (or green), medium, pockets
5. blue (or green), medium, water bottle
6. blue (or green), medium, key chain
7. blue (or green), medium, lunch bag
8. blue (or green), large, pockets
9. blue (or green), large, water bottle
10. blue (or green), large, key chain
11. blue (or green), large, lunch bag

Page 38
Sample answers:
1. How much do the items cost?
2. How many kids are going on the field trip?
3. How many plums and peaches did Garth pick?
4. How many jellybeans were in the bag?
5. How many pots does Cerise have?
6. What was Guy's spelling score?

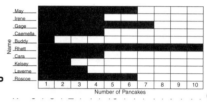

1. = 47 pancakes
2. 47 divided by 10 = 4.7
3. The mean is 4.7 pancakes.
4. 10 + 1 = 11 divided by 2 = 5.5
5. The median is 5.5 pancakes.
6. The mode is 4 pancakes.

Page 40
1. C
2. C
3. C
4. B
5. B
6. B
7. A
8. A
9. B
10. C

Page 41
1. A
2. C
3. B
4. A
5. A
6. C
7. A
8. C
9. A

Page 42
1. B
2. C
3. A
4. C
5. B
6. B
7. A
8. D

Page 43
1. C
2. B
3. C
4. B
5. B
6. A
7. B
8. B
9. A
10. B

Page 44
1. B
2. A
3. A
4. C
5. A
6. B

Page 45
1. C
2. B
3. B
4. B
5. C
6. A
7. A
8. A